Mimi Smith

Steel
Wool
Politics

Judith Tannenbaum

Institute of Contemporary Art
University of Pennsylvania

Exhibition dates:
February 4–April 17, 1994

The exhibition *Mimi Smith: Steel Wool Politics*
and this catalogue have been made possible by
grants from the Institute of Museum Services,
a federal agency; the Pennsylvania Council
on the Arts; the City of Philadelphia, and by
contributions from the friends and members
of the Institute of Contemporary Art.

Design: Diane K. Becotte
Printing: Becotte & Gershwin, Inc.
Horsham, Pennsylvania
Editing: Gerald Zeigerman

Cover: *No*, 1991
Paper, ink, ribbon
25 x 22 x 2

Inside cover: *November 24, 1978,
"The Eleven O'Clock News"* (detail), 1979
Colored pencil, graphite,
ink on black paper
30 x 40

Photography credits:
Oren Slor: cover, 4, 13, 16, 17, 20, 21, 22,
23, 24, 35
D. James Dee: inside cover

Dimensions are in inches unless otherwise
indicated; height precedes width precedes depth.

Foreword
Patrick T. Murphy

The Institute of Contemporary Art is delighted to present the work of Mimi Smith. Spanning the midsixties to the present, this survey features a number of pieces not previously exhibited—among them, seminal clothing sculpture that presages the current exploration of the genre by artists of a new generation. Utilizing the contents of the home and work environment, Smith has also been startlingly prescient in her anticipation of feminist criticism and environmental issues as well as the ways in which the media pervade our experience. Her critique exposes the coded messages within the seemingly innocuous objects and events of everyday life. Smith's approach is strikingly matter-of-fact, underscoring the inseparability between far-reaching public policies and our mundane private lives.

I wish to thank ICA's associate director, Judith Tannenbaum, for bringing this artist to our attention and presenting the work to a broader audience. Her essay not only documents Smith's concerns and obsessions but argues her significance in the development of political art that is both conceptual and activist.

We are grateful to Jane Carroll, ICA's registrar, for skillfully handling the many logistical demands of the exhibition, and William Rumley, our preparator, for his contribution to its planning and installation. Thanks are also extended to Diane Becotte for the sensitive design of this publication, Gerald Zeigerman for editing the text, and Francine Jaskiewicz for her research assistance.

We are most fortunate to enjoy the support and enthusiasm of ICA's advisory board and its exhibition committee, headed by Ella B. Schaap. Our exhibitions program is sustained by generous grants from the Institute of Museum Services, a federal agency; the Pennsylvania Council on the Arts; and the City of Philadelphia.

Most of all, we are indebted to Mimi Smith for her participation in this project. Her good humor, intelligence, attention to detail, and tenacity are all reflected in the objects she has created and graciously agreed to share.

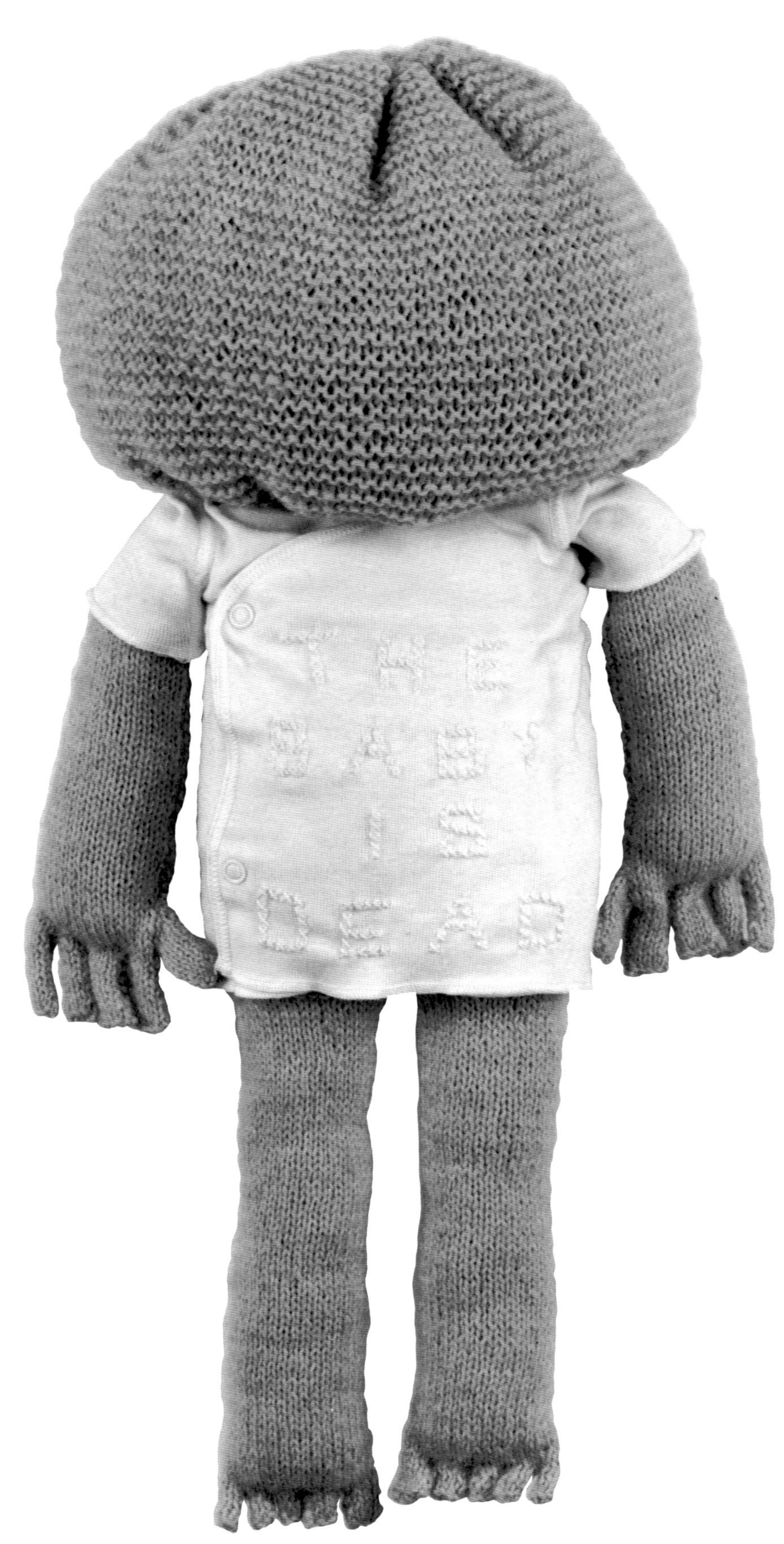

Knit Baby from
Knit Baby Kit, 1968
Yarn, undershirt
21 x 10 x 4

Mimi Smith: Quiet Radical
Judith Tannenbaum

Political art is not new, despite a burgeoning interest in visual objects designed to raise our consciousness about current social and political issues, nor does it have to be heavy-handedly didactic or polemical. Mimi Smith is an artist with a deadpan wit whose work thoughtfully and methodically connects mundane everyday experiences with broader political issues. She underscores how public policies impact directly on our daily activities and personal lives—ranging from the shape of the clothes we wear, the air we breathe, and the diseases we get to the radio and television news we hear. Not only do Smith's objects—clothing, books, clocks, television screens, and computer images—comment on everyday activities but they are made out of the "stuff" of ordinary life—fabric, thread, ribbon, tape measures, bath mats, tablecloths, steel wool, plastic wrap, candy, painters' dust masks—as well as more traditional art materials such as pencil on paper and paint on canvas.

Smith came of age in the sixties, a period marked by dramatic social change and turbulent political events—the civil rights marches, the assassinations of Malcolm X and the Kennedy brothers, anti-Vietnam War demonstrations, and the advent of the women's movement. It seems appropriate, therefore, that her work should become better known in the nineties, a period of renewed political activism. In 1963, she moved to New York from Boston, after graduating from Massachusetts College of Art. Having received traditional training in painting, the attitude at Rutgers University, where she subsequently entered the M.F.A. program, was, in contrast, one of great freedom and experimentation.[1] In addition to studying with Fluxus artist Robert Watts and sculptor-conceptual artist Robert Morris, she was exposed to the work of Roy Lichtenstein, Claes Oldenburg, George Segal, Lucas Samaras, and Allan Kaprow.[2] Jackie Winsor, Keith Sonnier, and Joan Snyder were graduate students in the same program.

Life in downtown New York combined with the nonideology at Rutgers that "anything could be art" proved so stimulating that by 1965 Smith was using clothing as both the subject and form of her art. For her M.F.A. show at Rutgers, in 1966, she produced a roomsize installation called *The Wedding* (p. 6), which one could not enter. It featured an unpretentious, clear plastic gown with a thirty-foot-long train made of plastic carpet runners and tablecloths attached to a dress form (the bride) and ending in two plastic-lace pillows. In Smith's written thesis, *Clothes As a Form,* she amplified the exhibition: "I am not against weddings or wedding gowns. I just do not think they should lie." She went on to say that although the wedding is a central ritual and primary event in a young woman's life, it is only one day. In contrast to the daily routines and realities of marriage, it becomes frozen in time—a memory in a plastic box. Finding appropriately poignant visual equivalents based on common experience to embody and expose the illusions, lies, and contradictions that inhibit and harm us, continues to underscore all of Smith's work.

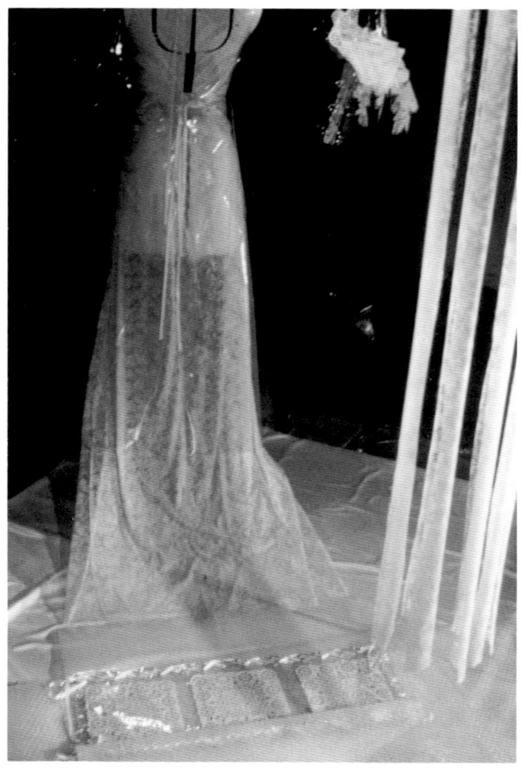

Train from *The Wedding,* 1966
Plastic carpet runners, plastic tablecloths, paper doilies, ribbon
30' x 4'

Smith's first clothes could be worn—for example, the remarkably prescient *Recycle Coat,* originally made in 1965 from the wrappings of paper towels and other household products (pp. 7, 13). Recognizing that an article of clothing carries layers of meaning and experience, she soon shifted to making clothes that were nonfunctional—that acted simultaneously as visual metaphor and sculptural object rather than wearable garment.[3] Smith honed in on feminine stereotypes in such objects as a greatly oversized vinyl *Bikini,* a contrastingly ultraslim *Model Dress,* and the outrageously large, heavy *Girdle,* made of rubber bath mats—implying that it is cruel to make women think they will achieve happiness through clothes, or forcing them to reshape their bodies so that others will find them attractive and admirable. Although her objects are carefully crafted, Smith used plastic, rubber, and other materials that deteriorate and discolor to address issues of vulnerability and impermanence; she also placed some pieces in plastic garment bags for protection.

Not only had Smith discovered in 1965 and 1966 that she could use nonart procedures and materials to make art, she took an even bolder position by using her autobiography and identity as a woman very concretely. Instead of concealing a woman's pregnancy in a shapeless tent, Smith's *Maternity Dress,* made of marbleized vinyl associated with sixties kitchen furniture, features a molded, clear plastic dome to reveal the growing baby. The extraordinary *Steel Wool Peignoir* (p. 17) combines soft pink nylon and lace with abrasive steel wool (surrogate fur), thus juxtaposing the seductive, romantic associations of the garment with the harsher aspects of marriage and a woman's daily chores. The *Knit Baby*, with instructions from 1968 (p. 4), is twenty-one inches long—the same measurement as her son, who was born in 1966. But the baby's featureless, stuffed form—with the words "the baby is dead" embroidered on its undershirt—also eerily embodies the artist's subsequent miscarriages before the birth of her daughter, in 1970.

In 1972, Smith moved to Cleveland, when her mathematician husband accepted a new position. Isolated in a strange city with two young children, for the next year and a half Smith made ghostlike, outlined versions of all the furniture and architectural features of her home—room by room (p. 8). Created to scale out of knotted thread and tape measures, the artist's obsessive method of endlessly tying knots is inseparable from the finished images of bureaus, kitchen appliances, windows, and other components installed directly on a wall. Unlike other "process art" and conceptual work of the period (practiced by Mel Bochner, Barry LeVa, Sol LeWitt, Dorothea Rockburne, and others), Smith wanted to use processes and subjects that related to her daily activities. One marvels at the pent-up energy compressed in the lines of these knotted string drawings as much as at the tedium of the process. Here, domestic life and art are indistinguishable.

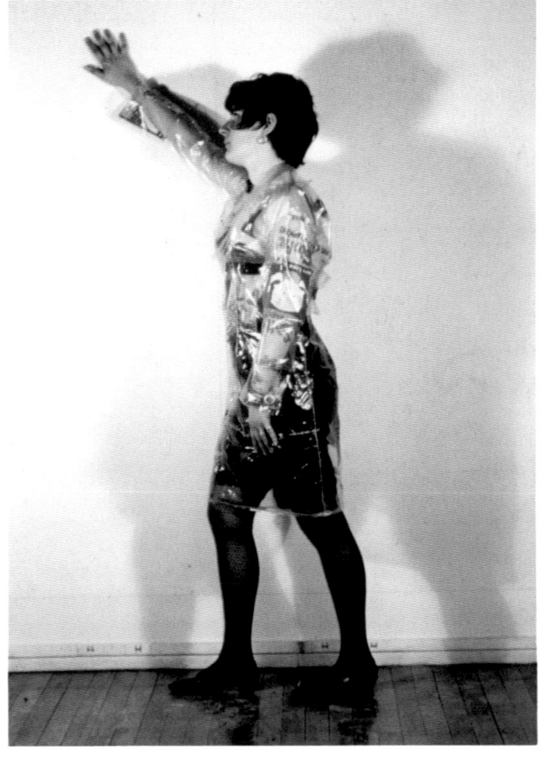

Recycle Coat, 1965
Plastic bags, plastic,
bottle caps
Worn by the artist

Smith's work became more overtly political in the late seventies and early eighties, focusing on events in the "outside" world in an extended series of ink, graphite, and colored pencil *Television Drawings,* often accompanied by audiotapes. The tense knotted line of the string drawings has changed into handwritten scripts transcribed from network news broadcasts. The methodical repetition and neutrality of Smith's appropriated written texts, which become synonymous with the shape and image of the television screen, represent another perfect match

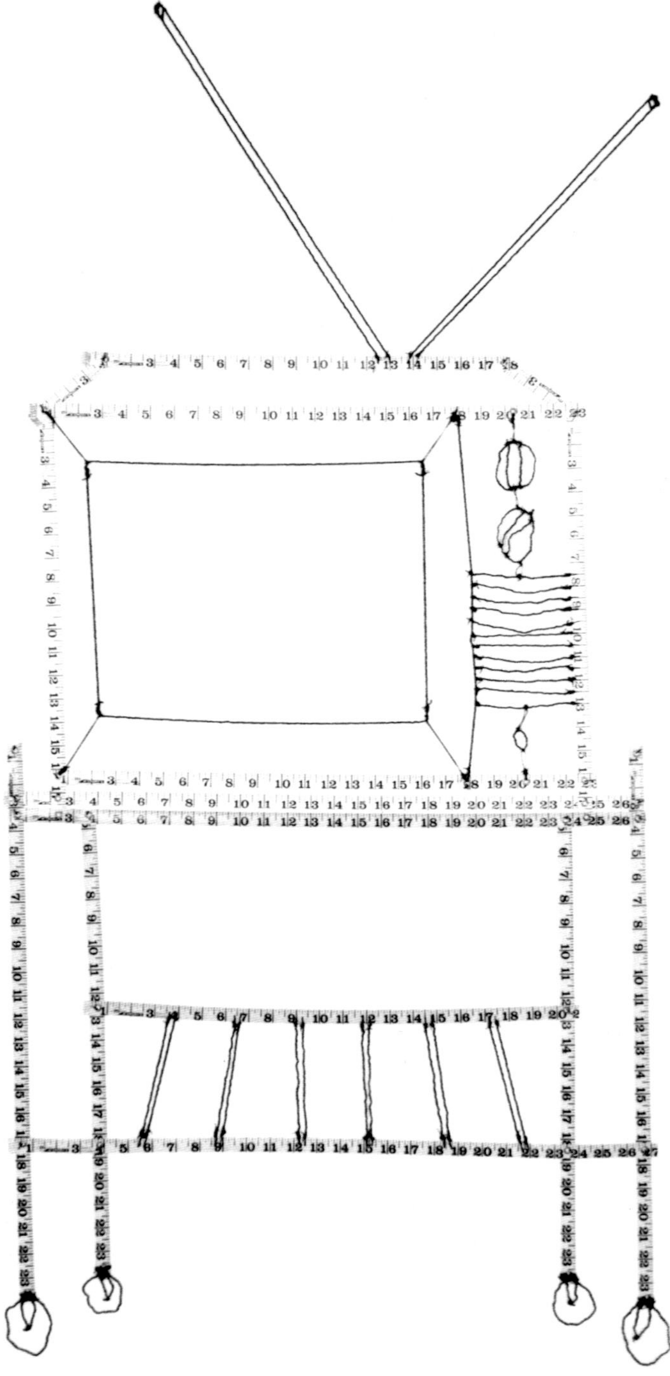

TV , 1974
Knotted thread,
tape measures
58 x 28

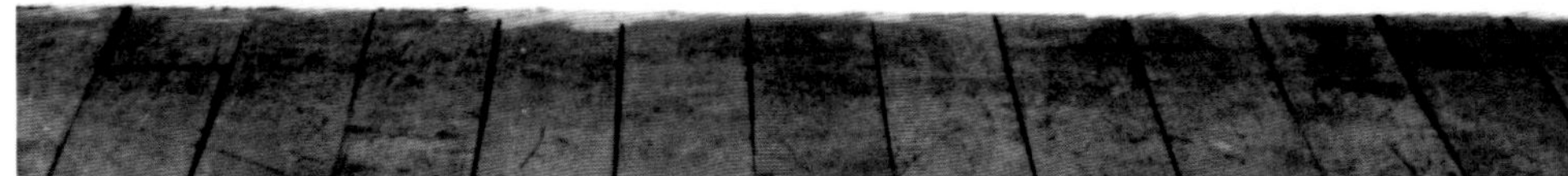

of form and content. Smith makes us see—and hear—the contrast between the droning background "white noise" of the newscaster's expressionless words (embodied in her repetitive script) and their all-too-often sinister or bizarre messages. Thus, major catastrophic events and personal tragedies may become confused with banal weather forecasts and traffic reports.

Emphasizing her intention to use information and experiences to which we all have access—whether it be shopping for clothes or watching TV—Smith states, "I believe that television is the most universal visual instrument of our time. It is looked at by more people for longer periods of time than any other object. This constant presence of television, its influence and intrusion into every life create a common experience across all economic and social lines." [4] *House with Clouds* (p. 10), a 1980 installation of word drawings and multiple-voice audiotapes, shows how television floods us with information, making it harder to shield ourselves from outside events. Here we see Smith as an environmentalist, focusing her attention on pollution. Messages about the effects of pesticides, pollution, and radiation on average middle-class citizens are spelled out on the four facades of the freestanding but vulnerable ten-foot-high paper house. Two TV news drawings float behind the windows on one facade: one drawing reports about the Three Mile Island nuclear reactor crisis (which had recently occurred), while the other quotes from a public-television documentary about the devastating physical effects of pesticides. The audiotapes emanating from inside the house continuously echo the written messages and chant pleas to take dangerous substances away from the house, thereby adding noise pollution to the already endangered domestic environment. The cloud drawings on the walls underscore how nature and culture are interconnected by pollution.

World events and public policies continue to invade Smith's studio and home—and our interior spaces, as well. In a more recent installation, *Nuclear Family* (p. 16),

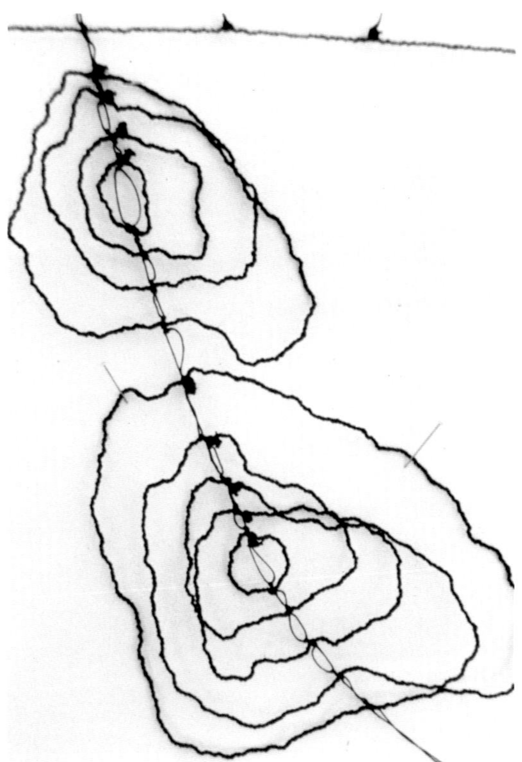

Stove (detail), 1973
Knotted thread
53 x 31

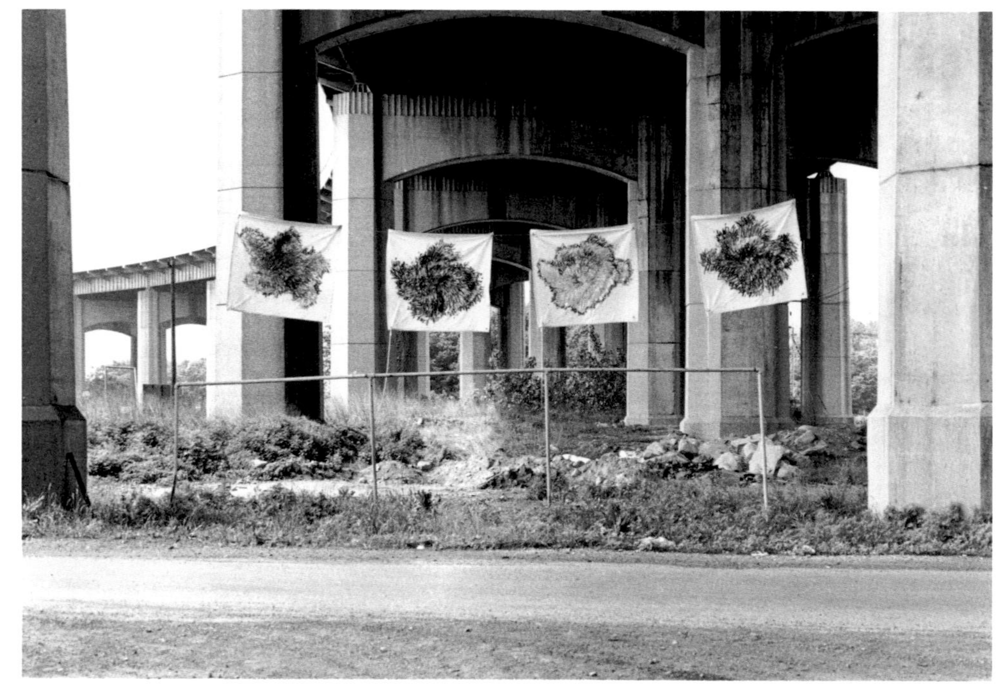

Polluted Clouds, 1979
Outdoor installation
under the Triborough Bridge,
Wards Island, New York City
Oil stick on sailcloth
5' x 5' each

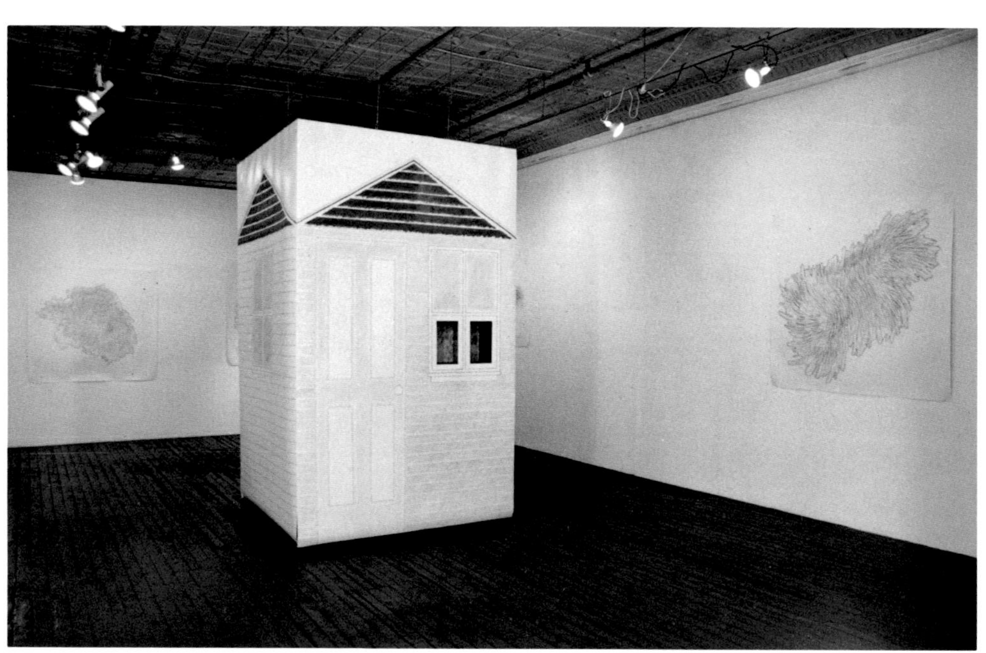

House with Clouds, 1980
Installation at 55 Mercer Street,
New York City
Pencil, ink, oil stick on paper
House: 10' x 6' x 6'
Clouds: 5' x 5' each
3 audiotapes

begun in 1986 but finished in 1993,[5] the painted house—whose composition features basic computer programming language used ironically to tell a story in English with such words as "home," "normal," "end," "delete"—is threatened by nuclear disaster. Each of the four generic family members—man, woman, boy, girl—is represented by a simple garment covered in house painters' dust masks, which would be highly inadequate protection in the event of an environmental or nuclear emergency.

By the mideighties, Smith shifted her focus from the television set to the computer—the latest widespread technology to alter our daily lives profoundly. Again, the artist uses both the image of the machine and its technological language to explore the subliminal messages it conveys. Computer graphics programs generate abstracted digitized images, but most striking are the "error messages" that come up inadvertently on computer screens, and which Smith has turned into the subject matter of several series of paintings (p. 19). Psychological fear and terror are unexpectedly far-reaching in such messages as "fatal error," "press escape," "out of memory," "incompatible," and numerous others that we may disregard in our daily work. Computer error messages have stimulated several recent clothing installations, including *Slave Ready (Corporate)* (p. 20), featuring a woman's pinstripe suit trimmed with steel wool and presented with a small computer-screen painting and clock, and *To Die For?* (p. 21), a camouflage patterned dress trimmed with lace that was made in response to the Persian Gulf War and recognizes the mixed blessing of women's increased role in the military.

Smith's understanding of how private lives are inextricably and profoundly connected to public issues led to a number of projects designed for spaces outside traditional art galleries—among them, city street windows, subway stations, corporate lobbies, and hospital grounds (p. 10). In addition, she participated in various Political Art Documentation/Distribution (PAD/D) projects,[6] Art against Apartheid, Artists Call against Intervention in Central America, and other political activities. When three of Smith's large television paintings were destroyed by a 1982 terrorist bombing of Chase Manhattan Bank, where they had been installed in a lobby project sponsored by the Lower Manhattan Cultural Council, Chase refused any liability. The artist found herself in a protracted real-life battle against the financial giant. Seven years later, a settlement for insurance compensation was reached.[7]

Books and clocks—two other common objects—have served as vehicles for Smith to express her social and political concerns since the seventies. Because of their small scale, their intimate connection with the reader, sequential format, and democratic orientation, books are ideal for fusing linguistic information with visual imagery (p. 18). In *This Is a Test* (p. 15), which combines the artist's preoccupations with mass-media and the threat of nuclear annihilation, her message is communicated through translucent overlays and the repetition of text and images. Smith transforms generic wall clocks with collaged images and written inscriptions to take on "timely" subjects ranging from abortion rights and gun control to the tragedy of AIDS (pp. 24, 25, 35). These working clocks always feature time as an idea as well as a mechanical component. Time is both the urgency and immediacy of the moment and the unrelenting march of history. As in all of her work, Smith's clocks poignantly transform everyday household objects, which are so familiar that we tend to disregard their meaning, into something uncommon that we cannot ignore.

In the nineties, Smith returned to clothing. In contrast to her early garments, which explored the "feminine mystique" and identity, recent works reflect women's roles in the workplace or address the need for protection—from environmental disasters or life-threatening illnesses. A recent group of steel wool *Coverings for an Environmental Catastrophe* (p. 22) include ambiguous forms designed to protect the face, torso, or pelvis while the larger *Chaps* (p. 23) and *Chest Plate* suggest such American male stereotypes as the cowboy and the baseball player. A new series called *Protectors against Illness* act as talismans to guard against specific diseases. The fragile pink bra with ribbons symbolic of breast cancer contrasts markedly with the witty, high-spirited *Candy Bra* (p. 26) Smith made of cellophane-wrapped hard candies twenty years earlier.

Smith does not shy away from difficult and painful subjects. In a new group of white paper cutouts of little girls' dresses, she takes on child sexual abuse. Simple, provocative words and phrases such as "No" and "She can't remember" undermine the purity and innocence of these paper dolls and force the viewer to confront a particularly disturbing social issue. Smith makes us see how everyday occurrences are not

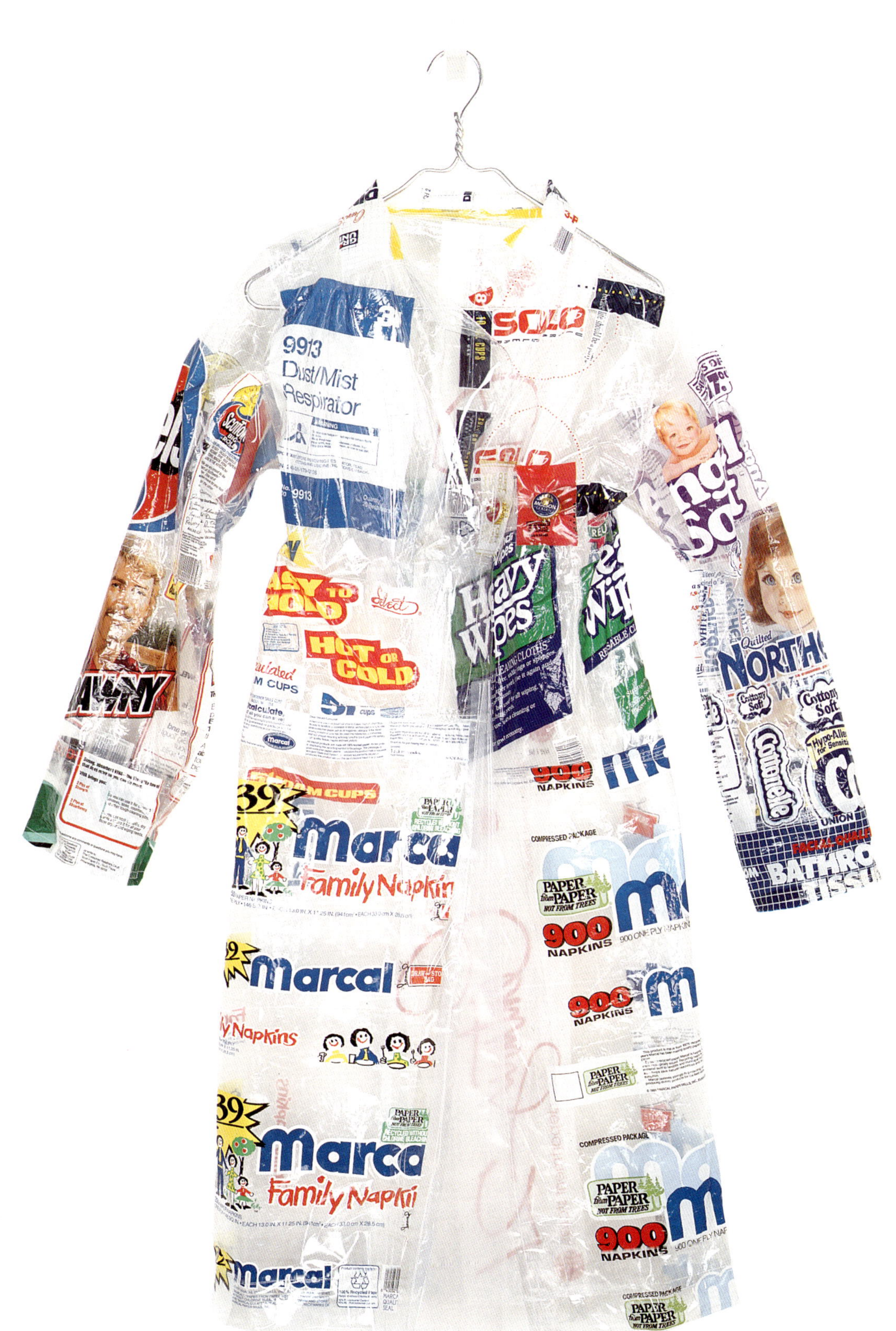

Recycle Coat, 1965/
remade in 1993
Plastic bags, plastic, bottle
caps, aluminum hanger
50 x 34

necessarily ordinary and, vice-versa, how seemingly unusual situations may be more common than we think.

In the past few years, a younger generation of artists has begun to explore the expressive and symbolic dimensions of clothing and shares Smith's interest in how garments embody stereotypes and expectations for women, as well as exploit their potential for drama. In our postmodern age, clothes become signifiers of identity—class, social status, ethnic group, sexuality. Smith's work is so poignant because her motivation comes not from a desire to critique our society but, instead, a need to transform her personal experience—as a woman of a certain generation and culture—into unique objects with which others may identify.

Notes

1. This essay draws on conversations between the author and the artist, from 1991 to January 1994.

2. Pop art, Happenings, neo-dada, and Fluxus performance work were all associated with the Rutgers and Douglass College art departments and artists living in the New Brunswick, New Jersey, area. In addition, Smith was very impressed when she saw Oldenburg's *Soft Toilet,* huge shirt, and transformations of other everyday objects and by Samaras's bedroom installation at the Green Gallery, in New York City. The violent edge, compulsiveness, and use of domestic subject matter in Samaras's work was a revelation.

3. In her thesis, *Clothes As a Form,* submitted in May 1966 in partial fulfillment of the M.F.A. degree, Smith addresses the specific roles of clothing, including protection, social conformity, economic/industrial generator, visual experience, psychological environment, fantasy, and symbolic identification with power.

4. From artist's statement in exhibition catalogue, A *Sound Selection: Audio Works by Artists,* organized by Artists Space, New York City, 1980.

5. Smith broke her wrist in an automobile accident in 1988 and was unable to execute work for the next eighteen months.

6. Smith worked for years with Barbara Moore and others organizing PAD/D's extensive archive of political art, which contains papers donated by Lucy R. Lippard, Dore Ashton, Rudolf Baranik, and numerous other political artists. The PAD/D archive is now part of special collections at the Museum of Modern Art Library, in New York City.

7. See Martin Fox, "Artist Suing for Lost Paintings Finally Gets Her Day in Court," *New York Law Journal* (May 8, 1989): 1-2; Jessie Mangaliman, "Art Issue: Who Pays for Bomb Damage?," *Newsday* (February 23, 1989): 23; and Walter Robinson, "Art World: Bank Pays on Blast Claim," *Art in America* (December 1989): 198.

Goodevening. Now here's the news. A nuclear bomb fell on Moscow today.. the Kremlin is a pile of rubble. the city is totally destroyed. It is not known what remains of the government. Millions are dead or dying. the living are dazed and in a state of shock and grief. the scenes of horror and also bravery were said to be unbelievable. In spite of the huge Soviet civil defense effort in the end there was no way to be prepared for what used to be the unthinkable. there are questions as to what kind of recovery will ever be possible from such disaster.

Page from *This is a Test,* 1983
Limited edition offset book
8¼ × 10¾

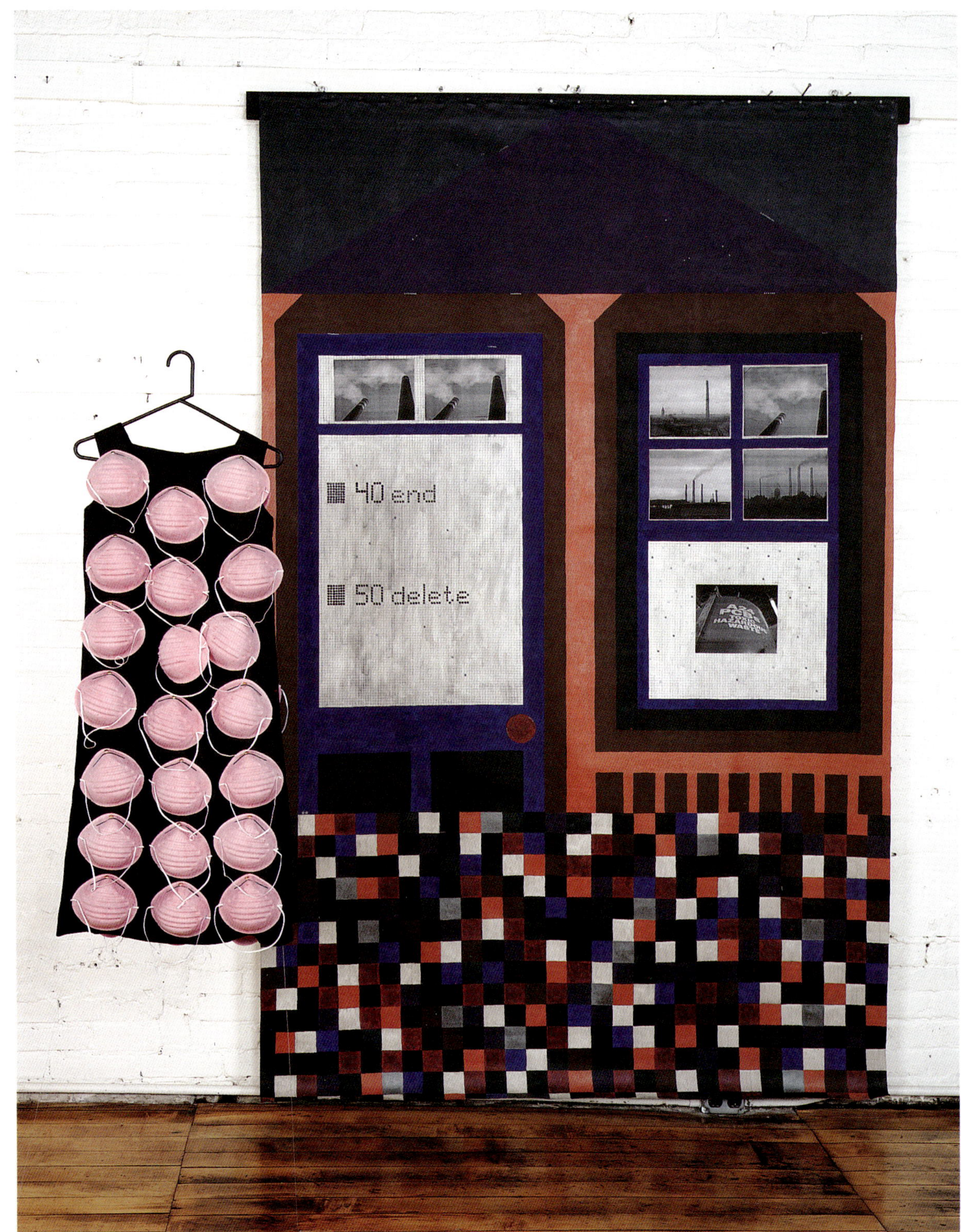

Nuclear Family
(detail), 1986–93
Painting: acrylic,
scanned computer
prints on canvas
96 x 60
Woman's Dress: rayon,
dust masks, steel hanger
47 x 21 x 7

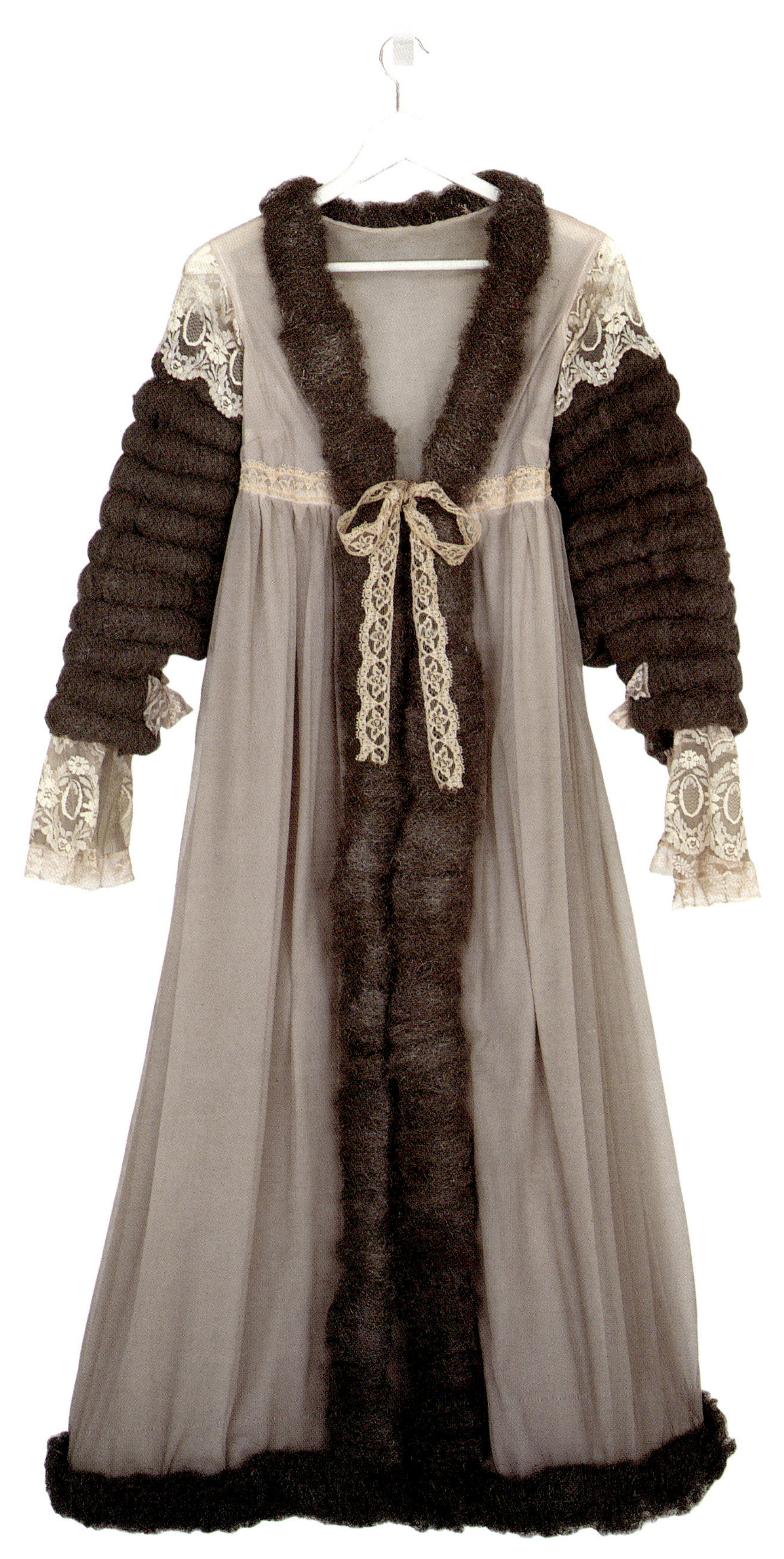

Steel Wool Peignoir, 1966
Steel wool, nylon, lace,
wood hanger
59 x 26 x 8

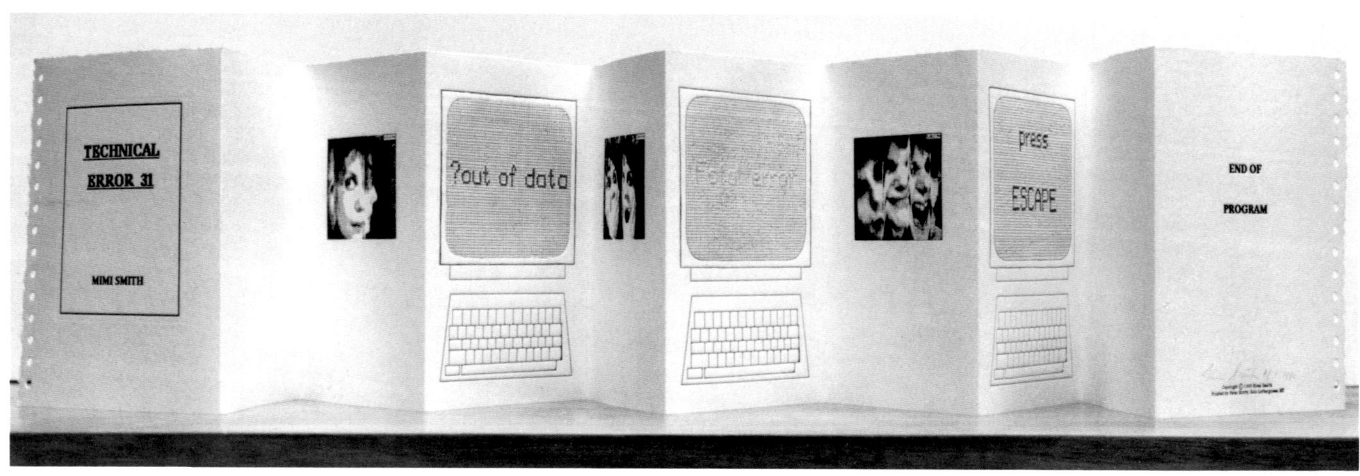

Technical Error 31, 1990
Limited edition book:
letterpress, paint on paper
8 x 50 open

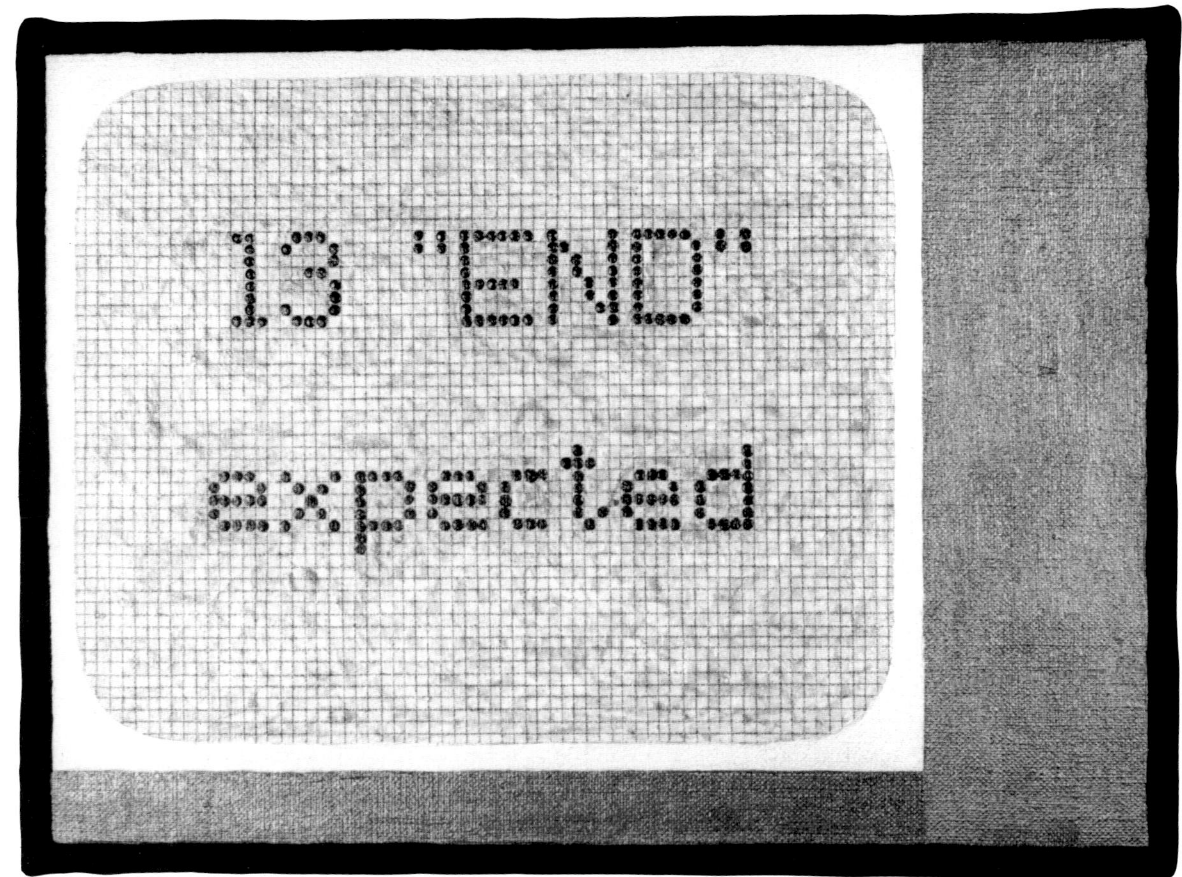

System Error 13, 1987
Acrylic, pencil on canvas
9 x 12

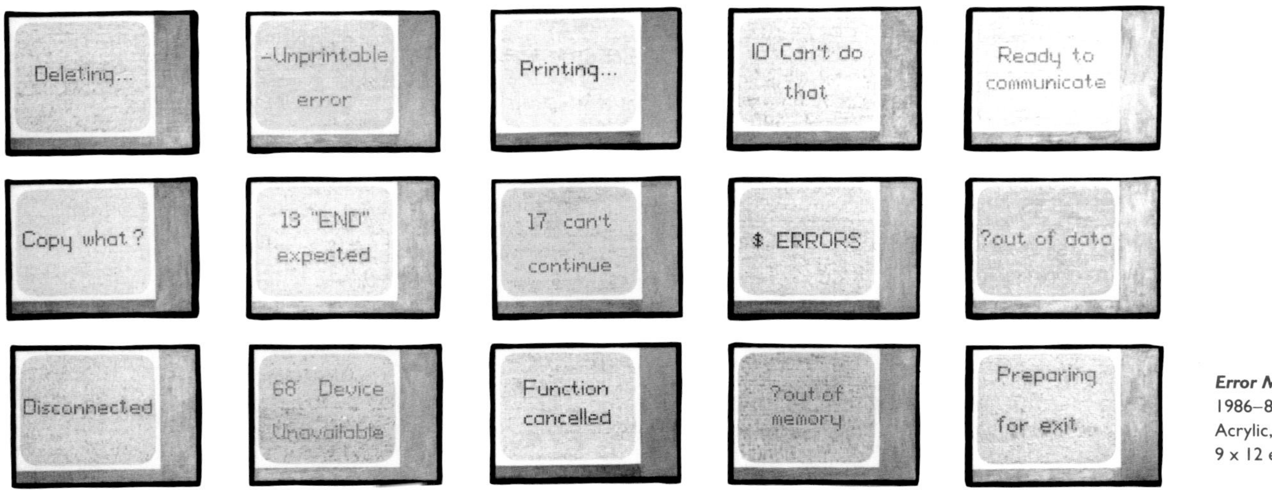

Error Messages 1–15,
1986–87
Acrylic, pencil on canvas
9 x 12 each

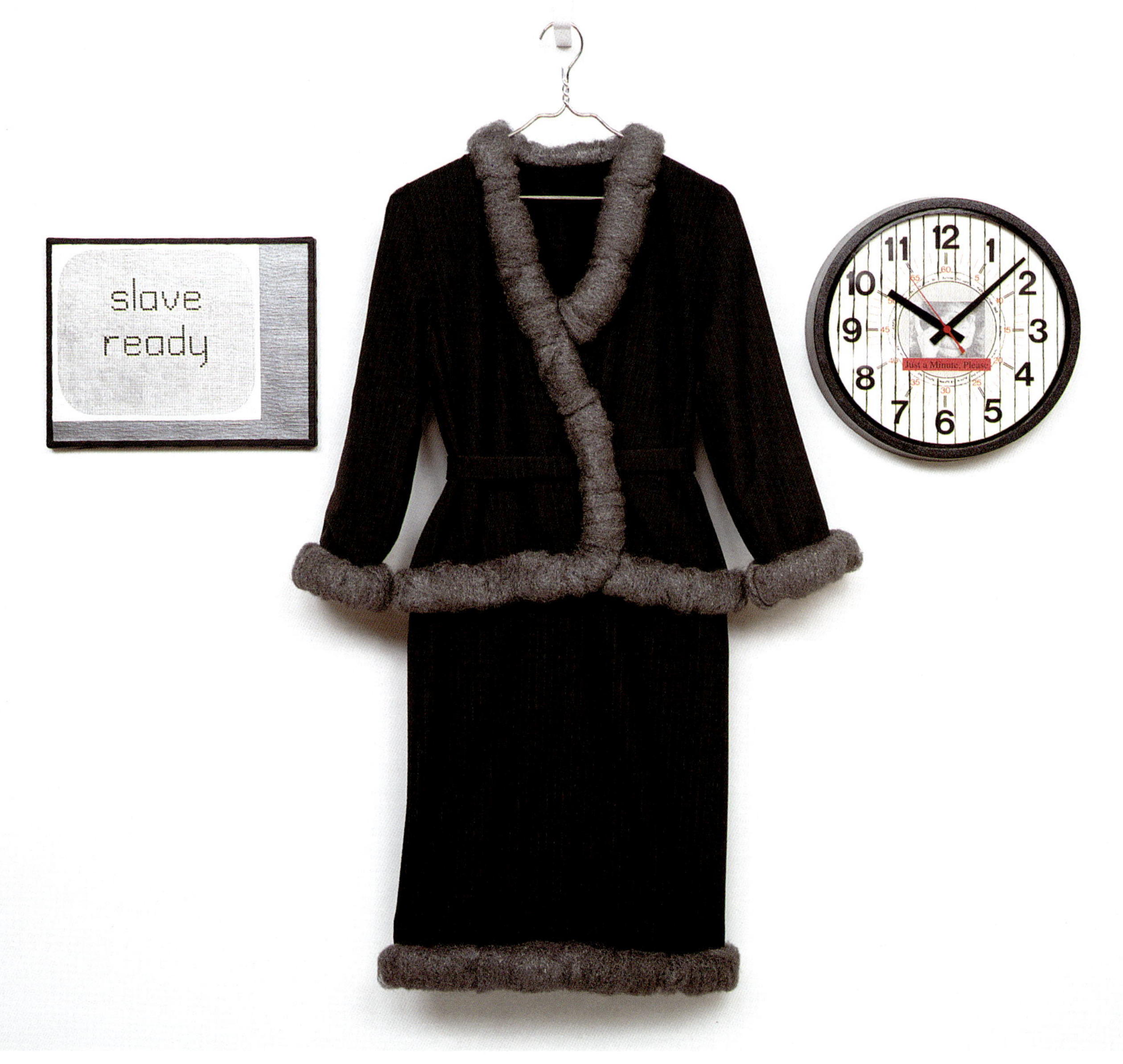

Slave Ready (Corporate), 1991-93
Suit: steel wool, pinstripe wool
fabric, aluminum hanger
Clock: acrylic, computer printout
on clock
Painting: acrylic, pencil on canvas
50 x 60 x 6 installed

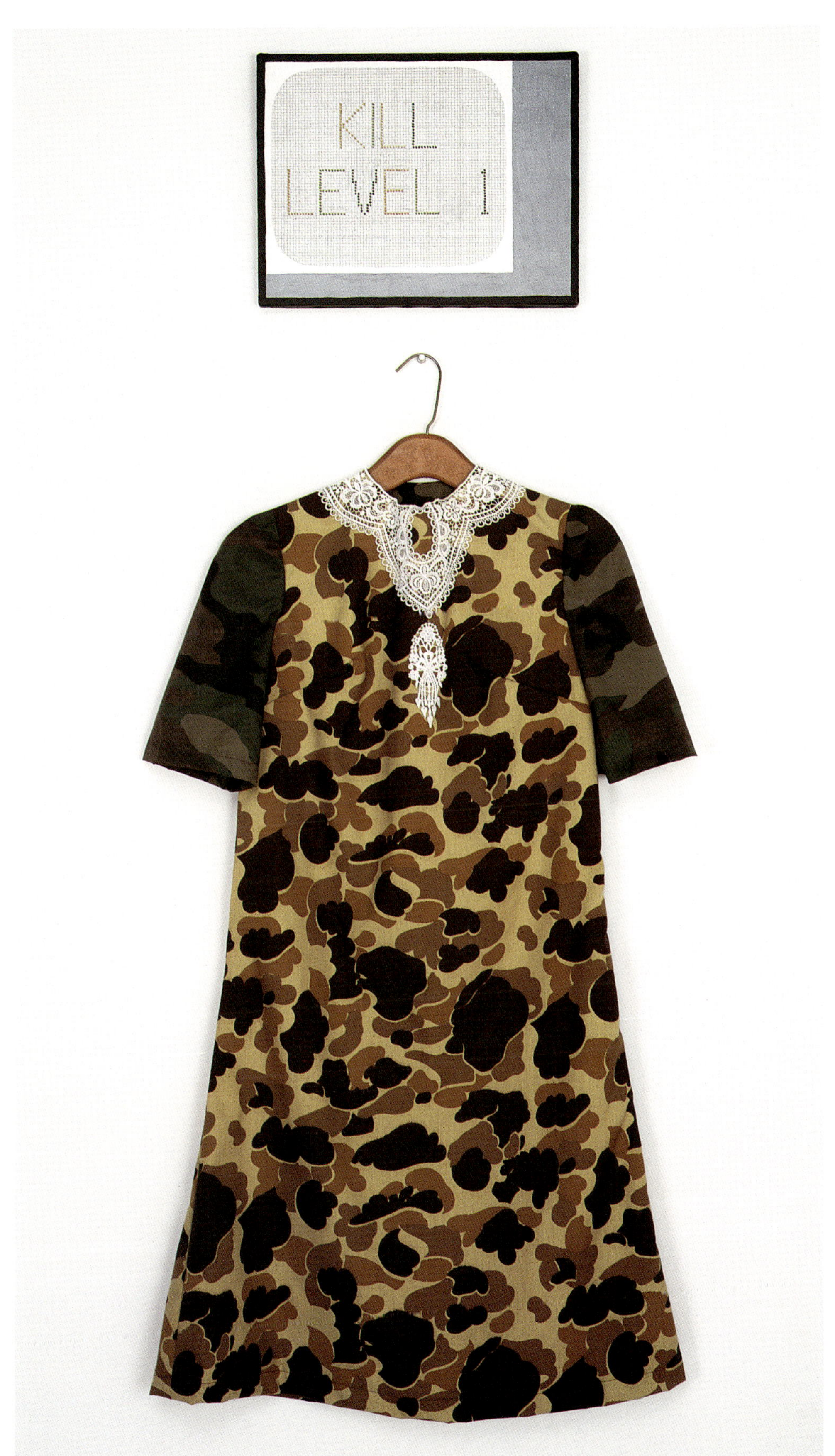

To Die For?, 1991
Dress: camouflage fabric,
lace, wood hanger
Painting: acrylic on canvas
60 x 24 x 6 installed

21

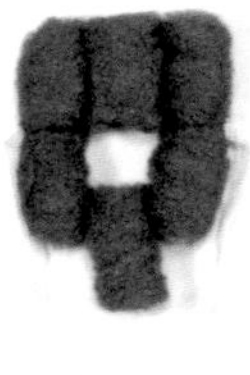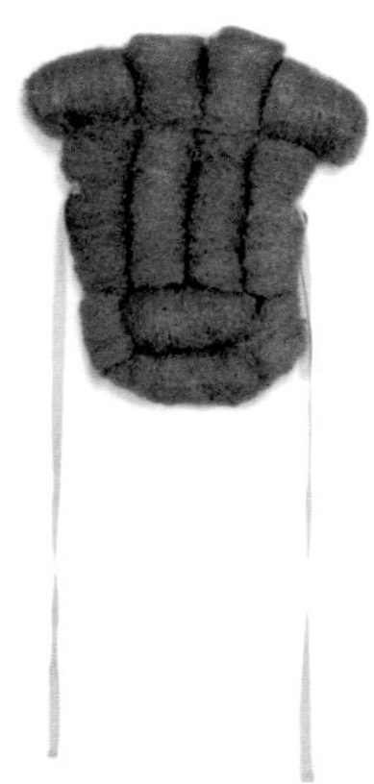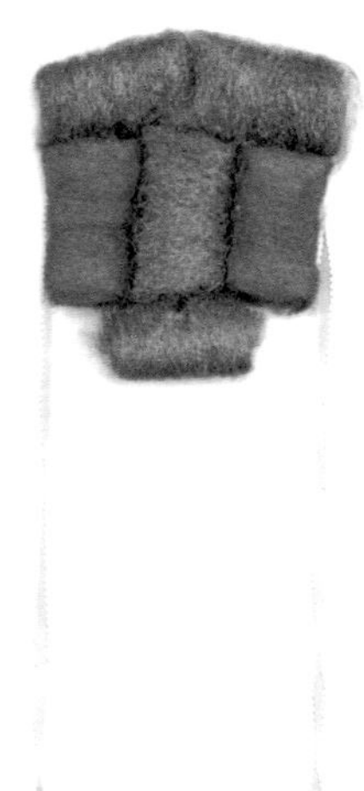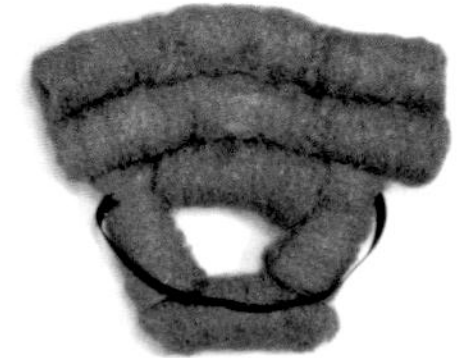

***Coverings for an Environmental
Catastrophe***, 1991
Steel wool, ribbon, elastic
11 x 7; 22 x 10; 26 x 10; 10 x 12

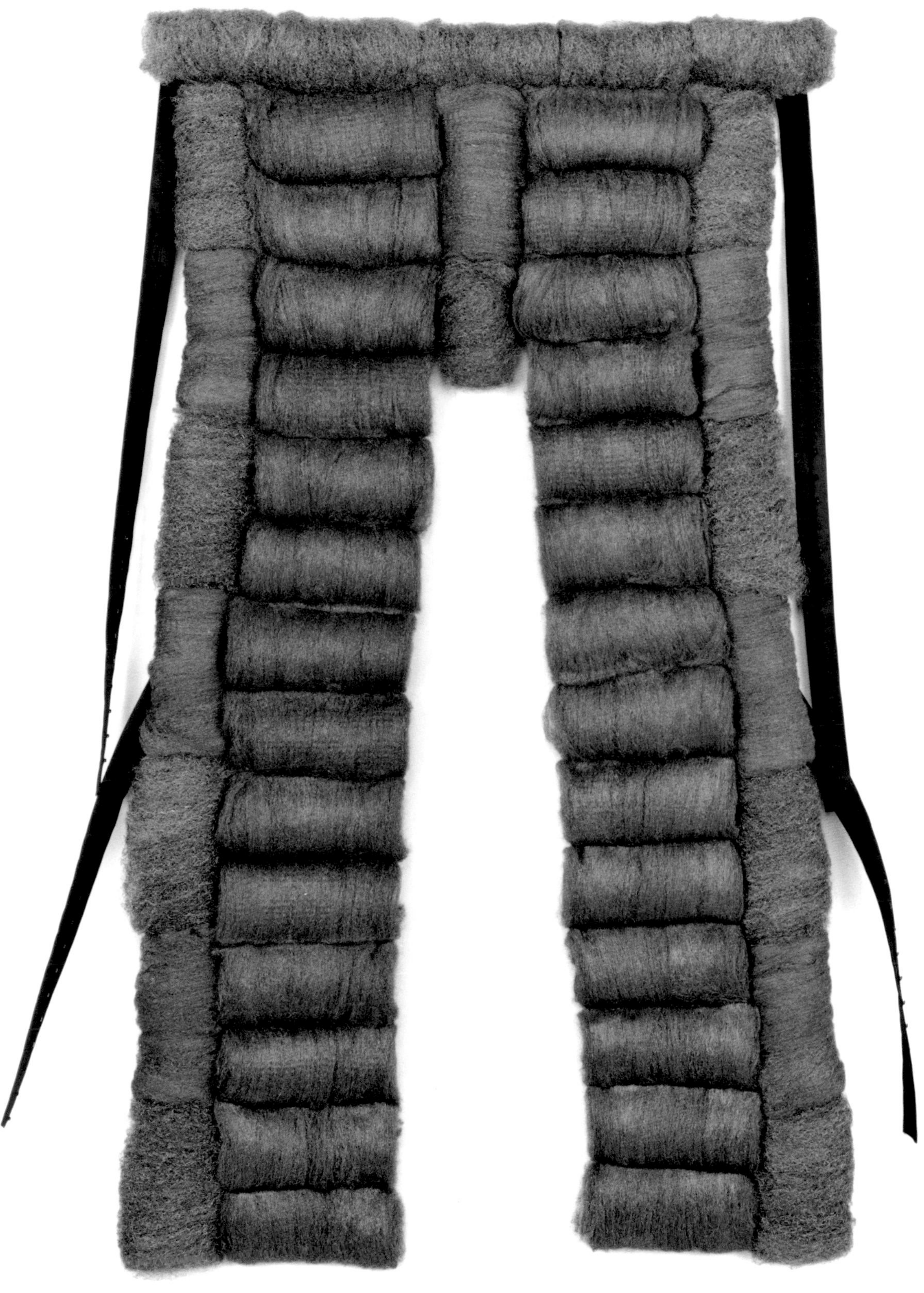

*Covering for an
Environmental Catastrophe:
Chaps*, 1992
Steel wool, aluminum
screening, fabric, hooks
38 x 26 x 3

23

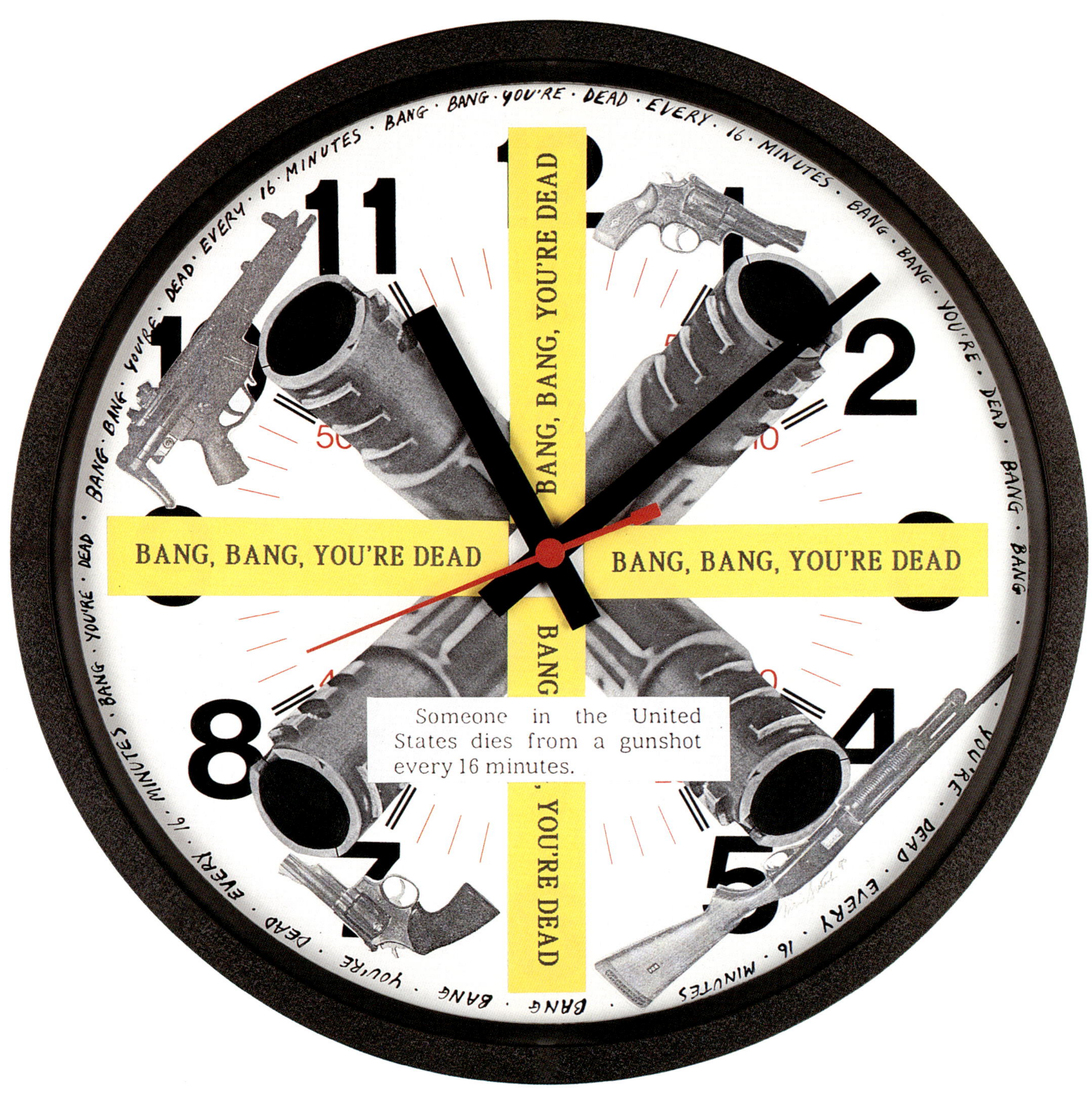

Bang, Bang, 1990
Acrylic, computer printout,
Xerox on clock
14 diameter

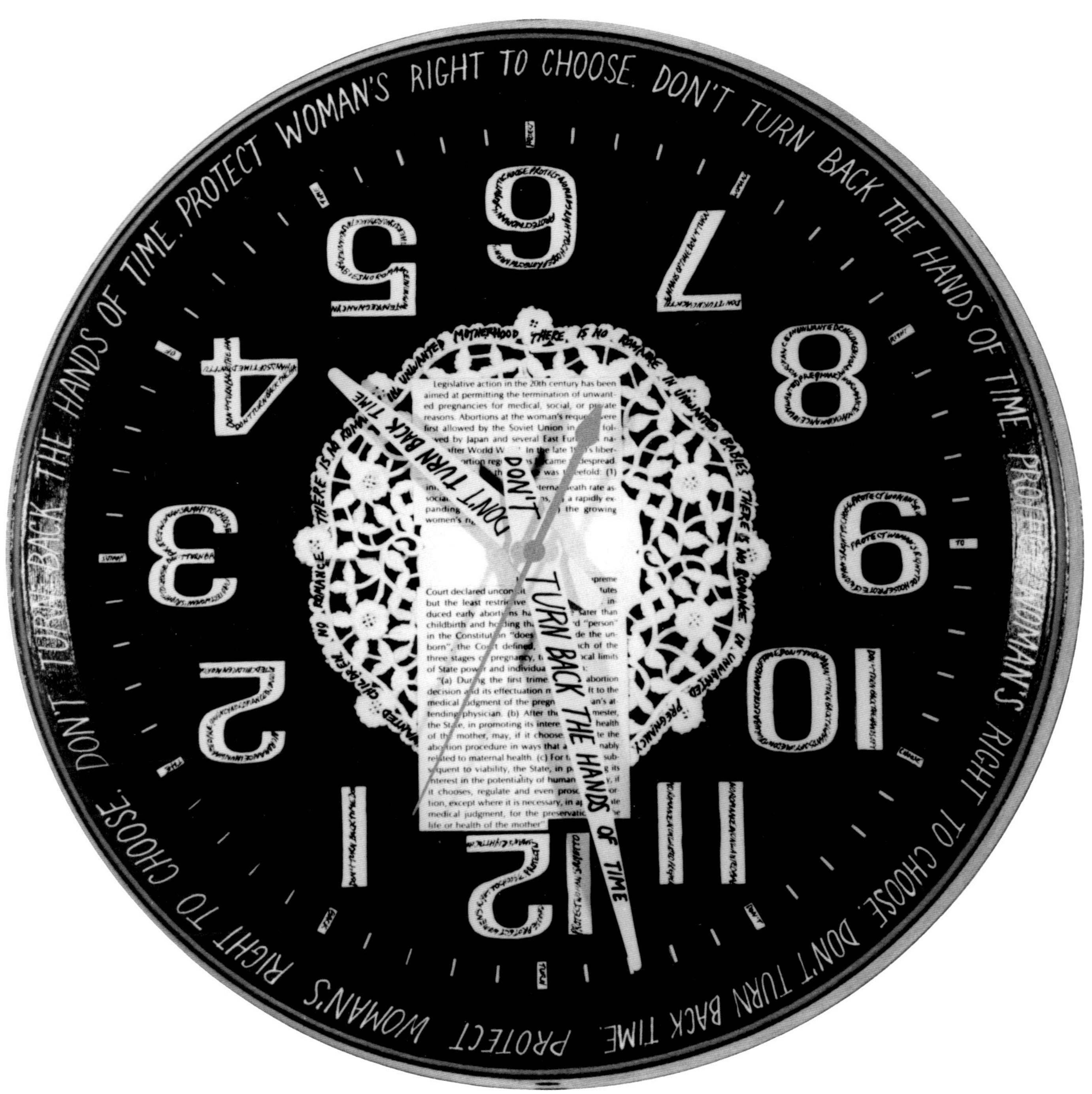

Don't Turn Back, 1985
Acrylic, paper,
Xerox on clock
14 diameter

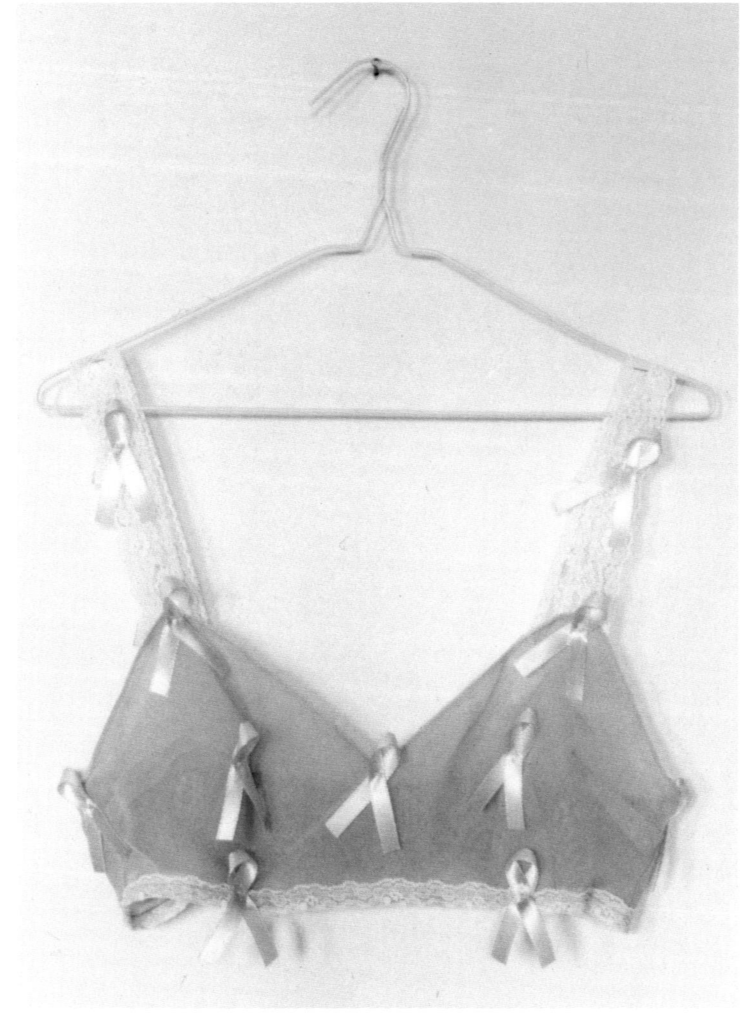

Protector against Illness:
Bra, 1993
Fabric, lace, ribbon,
metal hanger
18½ x 15

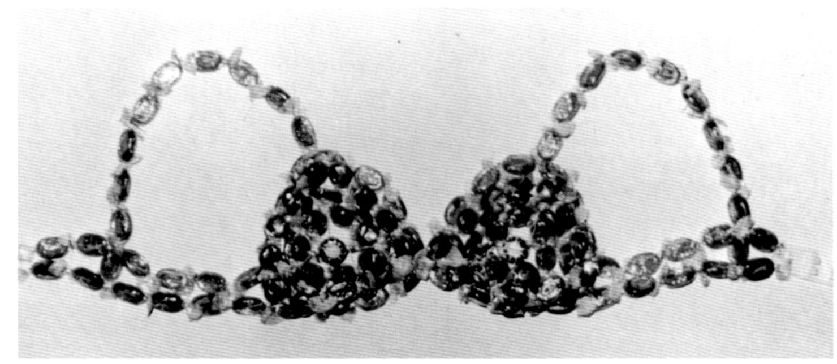

Candy Bra, 1972
Elastic, candy,
thread, hooks
11 x 34 x 2

Dimensions are in inches unless otherwise indicated; height precedes width precedes depth. All works are lent by the artist.

Recycle Coat, 1965/remade in 1993
Plastic bags, plastic, bottle caps, aluminum hanger
50 x 34

Bikini (for a large woman), 1965/remade in 1993
Plastic, wire
48 x 48, installed

Model Dress, 1965/remade in 1993
Plastic, buttons
72 x 24

Girdle, 1966
Rubber bath mats, elastic, ribbon, wood hanger
58 x 18 x 8

Maternity Dress, 1966
Plastic, vinyl, zipper, screws, wood hanger
45 x 20 x 9

Steel Wool Peignoir, 1966
Steel wool, nylon, lace, wood hanger
59 x 26 x 8

Train from *The Wedding*, 1966
Plastic carpet runners, plastic tablecloths, paper doilies, ribbon
30' x 4'

Knit Baby from *Knit Baby Kit*, 1968
Yarn, undershirt, handwritten instructions on paper
21 x 10 x 4

Jockstrap, 1972
Elastic, Tootsie Rolls, thread
10 x 18 x 2

Candy Bra, 1972
Elastic, candy, thread, hooks
11 x 34 x 2

Kitchen, 1973
Knotted thread
78 x 132 overall, includes:

Stove
53 x 31
Sink
53 x 47
Refrigerator
74 x 31

Bedroom, 1973
Knotted thread, tape measures
Includes:
   Bed
   72 x 60
   Bureau with *Mirror* and *Sconces*
   Bureau: 47 x 47
   Mirror: 27 x 17
   2 sconces: 7 x 4 each
   Chest of Drawers
   65 x 36

Living Room, 1974
Knotted thread, tape measures
Includes:
   Easy Chair
   72 x 54
   TV
   58 x 28
   Fireplace
   57 x 103 x 10

April 16, 1978, "The 11 O'Clock News," 1978
Colored pencil, graphite, ink on black paper
30 x 40

December 7, 1978, "The 11 O'Clock News," 1979
Ink, pencil on black paper
30 x 40

Stop Before It's Too Late: A View of the Bomb in Color, 1978-80
Book: colored pencil, ink on Xerox paper, cardboard
11 x 7 closed; 11 x 70 open
Clock: ink on clock
14 diameter

House with Clouds, 1980
House: 4 drawings
Pencil, ink, oil stick on paper
10' x 6' each; 10' x 6' x 6' overall

Clouds: 5 drawings
Pencil, ink, oil stick on paper
60 x 60 each
Television: 2 drawings
Colored pencil, pencil, ink on paper
18 x 23; 20 x 27
3 audiotapes

Once Upon a Time, 1981
Colored pencil, ink on paper,
audiotape
Book: 14¾ x 13 closed;
14¾ x 95½ open

Time Is Running Out, 1981
Acrylic, ink, Xerox on clock
14 diameter

This Is a Test, 1983
Book: offset printing with
flocked cover
8¼ x 10¾
Edition of 700
Published by Visual Studies
Workshop Press, Rochester,
New York

8:15, 11:02, 1983
Acrylic, colored pencil, Xerox
on clock
18 diameter

The Majority, 1984
Acrylic, paper on clock
14 diameter

Don't Turn Back, 1985
Acrylic, paper, Xerox on clock
14 diameter

Her Time, Their Money, 1986
Acrylic, paper on clock
14 diameter

Error Messages, 1986-89
12 paintings
Acrylic, pencil on canvas
9 x 12 each

Nuclear Family, 1986-93
3 paintings: acrylic, pencil, scanned
computer prints on canvas
96 x 60 each

4 garments: rayon, dust masks, steel
hangers
Woman's Dress
47 x 21 x 7
Boy's Shorts
24 x 15 x 7
Girl's Dress
29 x 18 x 7
Man's Overalls
63 x 17 x 7

Time Is Money, 1989
Acrylic, ink, computer printout, Xerox
on clock
10 diameter

The Days Are Long, 1989
Acrylic, computer printout, Xerox on
clock
10 x 10

Dead Before Their Time, 1989
Acrylic, computer printout, Xerox on
clock
14 diameter

By the Year, 1989
Acrylic, computer printout, Xerox on
clock
10 x 10

Racing against the Muck, 1989
2 drawings: Xerox, computer
printouts, ink on paper
12 x 27 each
Clock: acrylic, colored pencil, Xerox
on clock
14 diameter

Bang, Bang, 1990
Acrylic, computer printout, Xerox on
clock
14 diameter

You Only Live Once, 1990
Acrylic, computer printout on clock
14 diameter

Technical Error 31, 1990
Book: letterpress, paint on paper
8 x 6 closed; 8 x 50 open
Edition of 25
Published by Solo Press, New York;
printed by Peter Kruty

Slave Ready (Corporate), 1991-93
Suit: steel wool, pinstripe wool fabric,
aluminum hanger
50 x 29 x 5
Clock: acrylic, computer printout
on clock
14 diameter
Painting: acrylic, pencil on canvas
11 x 14
50 x 60 x 6 installed

To Die For?, 1991
Dress: camouflage fabric, lace,
wood hanger
46 x 24
Painting: acrylic on canvas
11 x 14
60 x 24 x 6 installed

*Covering for an Environmental
Catastrophe*, 1991
Steel wool, elastic
10 x 12

*Covering for an Environmental
Catastrophe*, 1991
Steel wool, ribbon
22 x 10

*Covering for an Environmental
Catastrophe*, 1991
Steel wool, ribbon
26 x 10

*Covering for an Environmental
Catastrophe*, 1991
Steel wool, elastic
11 x 7

*Covering for an Environmental
Catastrophe: Chest Plate*, 1991
Steel wool, aluminum screening,
ribbon
30 x 24

*Covering for an Environmental
Catastrophe: Chaps*, 1992
Steel wool, aluminum screening,
fabric, hooks
38 x 26 x 3

She Can't Remember, 1991
Paper, ink, ribbon
25 x 22 x 2

No, 1991
Paper, ink, ribbon
23 x 22 x 2

Paper Doll, 1993
Paper, ribbon
25 x 22 x 2

Protector against Illness: Undershirt, 1993
Fabric, vitamin pills, wood hanger
23 x 16

Protector against Illness: Bra, 1993
Fabric, lace, ribbon, metal hanger
18½ x 15

Protector against Illness: Mask, 1993
Fabric, ribbon
18 x 7½

Biography

1942 Born in Brookline, Massachusetts.

1963 Massachusetts College of Art, Boston, B.F.A.

   Moves to New York, where she currently lives and works.

1966 Rutgers University, New Brunswick, New Jersey, M.F.A.

Grants

1978 National Endowment for the Arts, Artist's Fellowship Grant.

1982 New York State Council on the Arts, Visual Artist Project Grant with Visual Studies Workshop, Rochester, New York.

1986 New York Foundation for the Arts Fellowship.

Exhibition History

Individual Exhibitions and Installations

1973 "The Bedroom," The New Gallery, Cleveland.

1975 Hundred Acres, New York.

   "Five Windows," 112 Greene Street Gallery, New York.

1976 Institute of Contemporary Art, Tokyo.

1977 Franklin Furnace, New York.

1978 "A Reading of Two Drawings," Franklin Furnace, New York. Performance.

   55 Mercer, New York.

   Doane Hall, Allegheny College, Meadville, Pennsylvania.

1979 55 Mercer, New York.

   Mabel Smith Douglass Library, Douglass College, Rutgers University, New Brunswick, New Jersey.

   "Good Morning Class," included in "Sound at P.S. 1," P.S. 1, Institute for Art and Urban Resources, Long Island City, New York. Special project room installation.

1980 "Mimi Smith: Television Drawings," The Art Center, Waco, Texas. Catalogue with essay by Paul Rogers Harris.

   55 Mercer, New York.

   "From the Newsroom," A.I.R. Gallery, New York. Performance and installation.

1983 Printed Matter, New York. Window installation.

1990 "Mimi Smith: Books and Small Objects," Bound & Unbound, New York. Catalogue with essay by Barbara Moore.

1993 Valencia Community College, Orlando, Florida. Catalogue with essays by Robin Ambrose and Mimi Smith.

1994 "Mimi Smith: Steel Wool Politics," Institute of Contemporary Art, University of Pennsylvania, Philadelphia. Catalogue with essay by Judith Tannenbaum.

Selected Group Exhibitions

1974 Artists Space, New York.

1975 "Soho," Baltimore Museum of Art.

   "Artists' Notebooks," Franklin Furnace, New York.

1978 Kathryn Markel Fine Arts, New York.

1979 "Word/Object/Image," Rosa Esman Gallery, New York.

"O.I.A Ward's Island," Ward's Island, New York. Organized by Organization of Independent Artists and Manhattan Psychiatric Center. Outdoor installation.

"Visual and Sculptural Bookworks." Organized by Franklin Furnace, New York. Traveled to Montclair Art Museum, Montclair, New Jersey.

"Artists' Books, U.S.A." Organized by Franklin Furnace, New York. Traveled to Seibu Museum, Tokyo.

1980 "A Sound Selection: Audio Works by Artists," Joseloff Gallery, Hartford Art School, University of Hartford. Organized in conjunction with Artists Space, New York. Traveled to Contemporary Arts Museum, Houston. Catalogue with essay by Barry Rosen.

"Pages Plus: Visual and Sculptural Bookworks." Organized by Franklin Furnace, New York. Traveled to Creative Arts Center Gallery, Nelson Gallery/Atkins Museum, Kansas City, Missouri; and Anderson Gallery, Virginia Commonwealth University, Richmond.

"Words & Numbers," Summit Art Center, Summit, New Jersey.

1981 "Regalia," Henry Street Settlement, New York.

"Bookworks: New Approaches to Artists' Books." Organized by Franklin Furnace, New York. Traveled to Walker Art Center, Minneapolis; University of Arizona Museum of Art, Tucson; University Art Museum, University of New Mexico, Albuquerque; and The Art Center, Waco, Texas.

1982 "Artists Protest," Pratt Manhattan Graphics Center, New York.

"Artists' Books: From the Traditional to the Avant-Garde," Archibald Stevens Alexander Library, Rutgers University. Catalogue with essay by Clive Phillpot.

"Art Lobby," Chase Manhattan Plaza, New York. Organized by Lower Manhattan Cultural Council.

"The Atomic Salon," Ronald Feldman Fine Arts, New York. Catalogue: *The Village Voice*, June 15, 1982.

"Dada Processing," Walters Hall Gallery, Rutgers University, New Brunswick, New Jersey.

1983 "Seven Women—Image Impact," P.S. 1, Institute for Art and Urban Resources, Long Island City, New York.

"Terminal NY: Preparing for War," Brooklyn Army Terminal, Brooklyn, New York.

"Day In/Day Out," Freedman Gallery, Albright College, Reading, Pennsylvania. Catalogue with essay by Carter Ratcliff.

"Re-tool, Computer Works by 9 Artists," Artisanspace, Shirley Goodman Resource Center, Fashion Institute of Technology, New York.

1984 "Art against Apartheid," Westbeth, New York. Traveled to DC37 (District Council 37 labor union gallery), New York.

"Center for Book Arts: The First Decade," Second Floor Gallery, New York Public Library, New York. Catalogue with essay by Francis O. Matson.

"Artists Call," P.S. 122, New York.

"Disarming Images: Art for Nuclear Disarmament." Organized by Bread and Roses, the cultural project of the National Union of Hospital and Health Care Employees, AFL-CIO, and Physicians for Social Responsibility, New York. Circulated by Art Museum Association of America. Traveled to Contemporary Arts Center, Cincinnati, Ohio; University Art Gallery, San Diego State University, California; Museum of Art, Washington State University, Pullman; and New York State Museum, Albany; among others. Catalogue with essay by Nina Felshin.

"Words—Pictures," Bronx Museum of the Arts, Bronx, New York.

1985   "Latitudes of Time," City Gallery, Department of Cultural Affairs, New York. Organized by Organization of Independent Artists.

"Disinformation," Alternative Museum, New York. Catalogue with essays by Noam Chomsky and Edward S. Herman.

1986   "Bookworks Invitational," Erie Art Museum, Erie, Pennsylvania.

"New Liberty Monuments," Newhouse Center for Contemporary Art, Snug Harbor Cultural Center, Staten Island, New York.

1987   "The Second Emerging Expression Biennial: The Artist and the Computer," Bronx Museum of the Arts, Bronx, New York. Catalogue with essay by Patric Prince and introduction by Luis Cancel.

"Women's Autobiographical Artists' Books," Fine Art Galleries, University of Wisconsin Art Museum, Milwaukee. Catalogue with essays by Pamela Zwehl-Burke and Leslie Fedorchuk.

"Heresies 10th Anniversary Exhibit," P.P.O.W., New York.

"Concrete Crisis," Exit Art, New York.

"About Time," Islip Art Museum, Islip, New York.

"Connections Project/Conexus," Museum of Contemporary Hispanic Art, New York.

1988   "Committed to Print," Museum of Modern Art, New York. Traveled to University Art Galleries, Wright State University, Dayton, Ohio; Peace Museum, Chicago; Glenbow Museum, Calgary, Alberta, Canada; New York State Museum, Albany; Spencer Museum of Art, Lawrence, Kansas; Newport Harbor Art Museum, Newport Beach, California. Catalogue with essay by Deborah Wye.

"Clockwork!" List Visual Arts Center, Massachusetts Institute of Technology, Cambridge. Catalogue with essays by Dana Fries-Hansen, Katy Kline, and J. T. Fraser.

"Baltimore Collects Twentieth-Century Illustrated Books from a Private Collection," Baltimore Museum of Art.

"The Arts of the Book," Rosenwald-Wolf Gallery, Haviland Hall, and Aronson Gallery, University of the Arts, Philadelphia. Catalogue with essay by Clive Phillpot and introduction by Eleni Cocordas.

"The Changing Face of Soho," Bleecker Street Station IRT #6, New York. Sponsored by Artmakers and Arts for Transit, New York.

1989   "Home Sweet Home," Sally Hawkins Gallery, New York.

"Images and Words, Artists Respond to AIDS," Henry Street Settlement, New York. Traveled to Painted Bride Art Center, Philadelphia. Catalogue with essay by Anthony Holbrook.

"Loaded," Blue Star Art Space, San Antonio, Texas. Catalogue with essay by Glenna Park.

"Mythic Moderns," Real Art Ways, Hartford.

"The Center Show," Lesbian and Gay Community Center, New York. Catalogue with essays by Rick Barnett and Barbara Sahlman.

1990   "Happiness Is a Warm Gun," Webo, New York. Organized by Zone.

"Television Apparatus," New Museum of Contemporary Art, New York.

"Words and Images with a Message," Women's Studio Workshop, New York. Catalogue with essay by Anita Wetzel.

1991   "Artists of Conscience: 16 Years of Social and Political Commentary," Alternative Museum, New York. Catalogue with essays by Lowery Stokes Sims, Lucy R. Lippard, Margot Lovejoy, Keith Morrison, and Luis Camnitzer, and introduction by Geno Rodriguez.

"Burning in Hell," Franklin Furnace, New York.

1992   "10 Steps," Muranushi Lederman, New York.

"By Any Means Necessary," Printed Matter, New York.

1993   "Women at War," Ledisflam Gallery, New York.

"The Rag Trade," InterArt Center, New York.

"Songs of Retribution," Richard Anderson, New York.

Bibliography

Articles and Reviews

Bass, Ruth. "Women at War." *ArtNews* (November 1993): 167.

Bentivoglio, Mirella. "New York al Femminille." *Gala International* (June 1980): 37-38.

Blair, Eileen. "At the Galleries." *The Villager* (March 1979): 15.

Blevins, J. "Dressing Up the Terminal Tower." *Cleveland Magazine* (January 1974): 81-82.

Flicker, Robin. "A Woman's Work Is Never Done." *Downtown* (December 16, 1987): 15A.

Forsling, Stephen. "Art Lobby." *Down Town* [published by Lower Manhattan Cultural Council] (February 1982): 1.

Fox, Martin. "Artist Suing for Lost Paintings Finally Gets Her Day in Court." *New York Law Journal* (May 8, 1989): 1-2.

Harrison, Helen A. "'About Time' Examines Approaches to Temporal Themes." *The New York Times* (March 1, 1987): LI Section.

Heresies (issue 20): 74-75, photograph.

Hess, Elizabeth. "Covert Action." *The Village Voice* (March 9, 1993).

Kay, Jane Holtz. "Timepieces from Sundial to Swatch." *The New York Times* (January 26, 1989): C12, photograph.

Kutner, Janet. "Art Alert . . . This Is TV . . . Tune Out . . . Your Minds." *The Dallas Morning News* (November 28, 1980): C1, C6.

Levin, Kim. "Choice Works." *The Village Voice* (February 12, 1985): 70.

———. "Let's Play House." *The Village Voice* (June 3, 1986): 66.

"Library Exhibits: Douglass Library." Rutgers Libraries Newsletter (1979): 10.

Linker, Kate. "NY Reviews, Art Lobby." *Artforum* (May 1982): 81-82.

———. "NY Reviews, Disinformation." *Artforum* (Summer 1985): 105-6.

Lippard, Lucy R. "Don't Bank on It." *The Village Voice* (March 2, 1982): 77.

Logermann, Jane, and Sandy Gellis. "Interviews: Art and Science." *Heresies* (issue 13): 44.

Lubell, Ellen. "Art Reviews." *The Soho News* (January 19, 1978): 27-29.

Mangaliman, Jessie. "Manhattan Closeup— Art Issue: Who Pays for Bomb Damage?" *Newsday* (February 23, 1989): 23.

Manganis, Julie. "Artists Strike a Timely Note." *The Boston Herald* (February 10, 1989): 26-27.

Mathewson, William. "Shop Talk: In a Very Special Sense, the Art Show Bombed." *The Wall Street Journal* (June 10, 1988): 25.

McDarrah, Fred. "Voice Choices." *The Village Voice* (January 2, 1978): 47.

Meinwald, Daniel. "Making Book." *Camera Arts* (July 1983): 8.

Moore, Barbara. "P.S. 1." *Express* (Winter 1984): 11.

Nadelman, Cynthia. "NY Reviews." *ArtNews* (May 1979): 182.

Perreault, John. "Clothes Call." *The Soho News* (December 23, 1980): 53.

Princenthal, Nancy. "Artist's Book Beat." *The Print Collector's Newsletter* (January-February 1991): 237.

Rice, Shelley. "Reviews, NY." *Artforum* (Summer 1980): 87-88.

Robinson, Walter. "Art World: Bank Pays on Blast Claim." *Art in America* (December 1989): 198.

Schwendenwien, Jude. "Dress Code: Clothing As Sculpture." *Sculpture* (November-December 1993): 26-31.

Softic, Tanja. "Mimi Smith: A Retrospective, 1966-1992." *Art Papers* (May-June 1993): 46-47.

Stein, Judith. "The Artists' New Clothes." *Portfolio* (January-February 1983): 62.

Books and Other Publications

Lyons, Joan, ed. *Artists' Books: A Critical Anthology and Sourcebook*, Gibbs M. Smith, Inc., Peregrine Smith Books, in association with Visual Studies Workshop Press, 1985:

"The Artist's Book Goes Public," Lucy R. Lippard, 52, 54; "Words and Images: Artists' Books As Visual Literature," Shelley Rice, 76-78.

Published Articles by Mimi Smith

"Art Careers and an A.I.R. Panel." *Women Artists Newsletter* (November 1977): 2.

"Conversations and Reminiscences: My Grandmother's Pictures." *Heresies*, issue 4 (1978): 87.

"Peignoir and Girdle." *Heresies*, issue 6 (1978): 36.

"The Met As Alternative Space." *Women Artists News* (June 1978): 7.

Books Published by Mimi Smith

This Is a Test. Rochester, New York: Visual Studies Workshop Press, 1983. Offset printing, edition of 700.

Technical Error 31. 1991. New York: Solo Press; printed by Peter Kruty, 1991. Letterpress with hand painting, edition of 25.

Radio Broadcast

Morris, Diane. "Disinformation." *WBAI* (March 29, 1985).

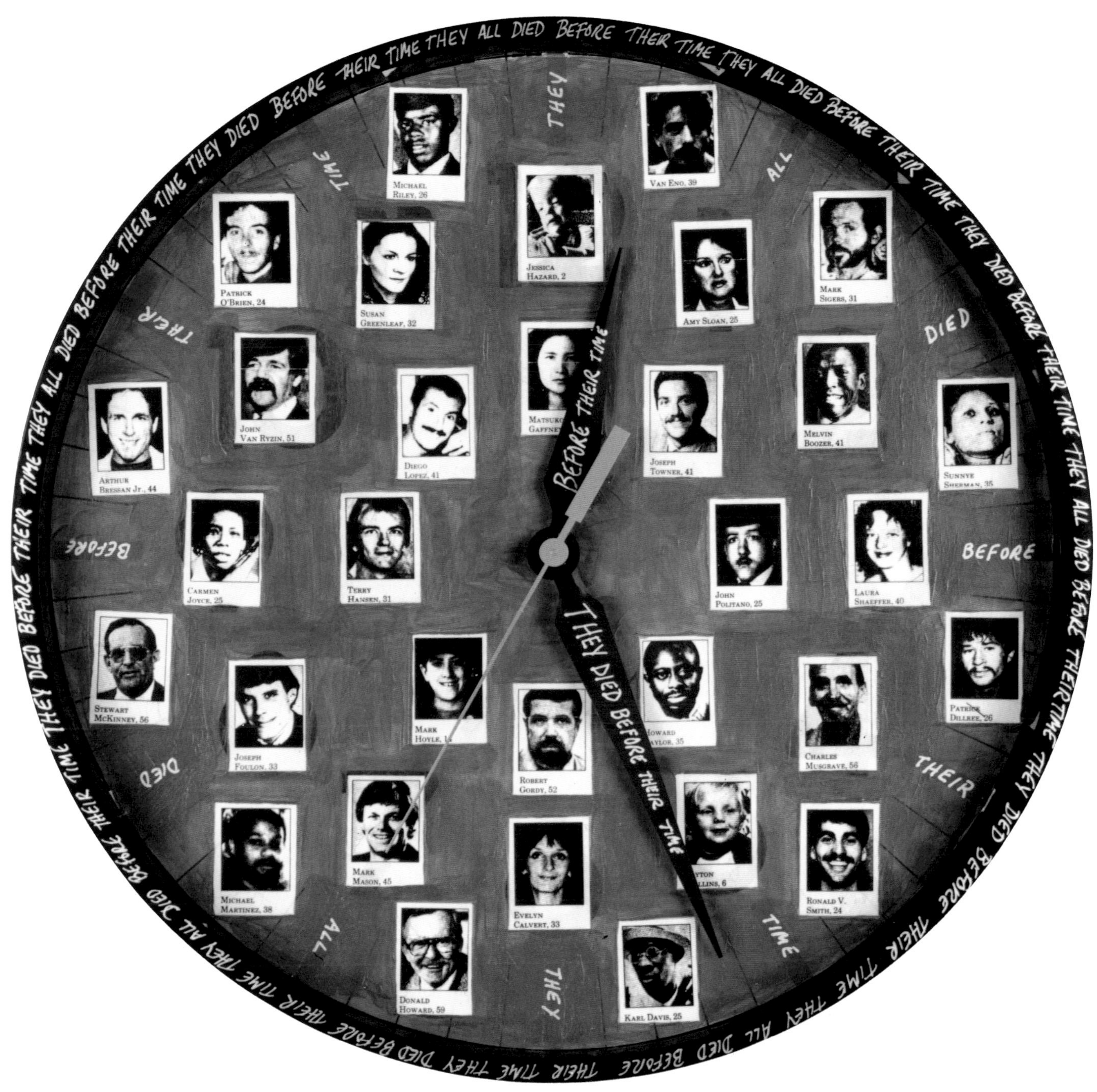

Dead Before Their Time, 1989
Acrylic, computer printout,
Xerox on clock
14 diameter